HIDDEN EMOTIONS

STUFFED FEELINGS IN A SHADE OF FIFTY

ADHYA

Made with ♥ on the Notion Press Platform
www.notionpress.com

With love,

Dedicated to myself, my endless journeys filled with ups and downs. My younger sister, who has always been with me when needed and my bestfriends without whom i never knew how to smile again.

My parents, I love you both, always and forever.

Contents

Contents

Contents

Preface

Writing poems is like a hobby of mine. For many years I have been writing seas of poetries filled with endless mysteries. The poems i have written describes my emotional state, the way i felt back then, be it joy or sorrow, happiness or depressed, the literature flashes it well. As i am a teenage girl, these poems will definitely soothe or calm down the nerves of many teenagers.

1. Promise

The days of sweet dreams
Can never be capable to suffice
My tenderness for you
The blaze burns with avarice.
Under the magnificent tree
I hold it with true humane
Sharing my feelings for you
That rapidly drives me insane.
One promise I would make to you
To care and nourish you,
To never leave your side,
Just to assure you.
One promise I would make,
to hold you up in your deed,
Just like the crack of dawn,
stand to fight for you in need.
One promise I would make you clear,
Just you are my endear,
and keep it in mind my love
My relish proclivity
It's all you, I swear.

2. May you be missing

Days are passing like sand
Missing the intermingling of our hand
Suffering a lot what to say
Missing your arms to gently lay.
Sometimes I may be mad
And fragile and vulnerable
But you have to handle
And should make me a little stable.
Maybe I'm weak and shy,
But I care for you far and nearby
I love you with my soul heart
And swear never told you a lie.
I may become angry
And feel helpless for future
May fear to lose all contacts
And the love you still nurture.
Because my heart is of glass
Pure and can be shattered with a slash,
I maybe wrong but,
Only you have the power to trash.
May you be feeling the same
Missing me igniting flames,
Terribly falling and wondering in Lanes

But upset, alone, waking in pain.
May you be missing
Me the way, I am suffering
May you be feeling
Me the way I am dealing
May you be weeping,for
Me as I am crying,
May you be staring
The empty walls, searching
Me, the way I'm dying,
May you be missing.

3. Blizzard

I remember those days
When we used to laugh and talk
I remember those moments
When we were free, supported by luck.
Unforgettable hopes and requests
We prayed to lord in secret
No nothing helped then,
For us, to integrate.
Growing the needs and desires
Wildly like blaze of fire,
Dying without you,
Like hollow as you are my air.
Nothing can fulfil it
By leaving you far from me,
I know it is hard,
Passing days without glee.
Although knowing the realities,
I fear to down my desire,
Remembering the magnificent days
Burning like a blizzard of fire.

4. Sinister-you

At last you had hollowed,
My innocence you just blowed
The magnificent cruelty,
I burnt the ashes that you shoved.
Tell me my fault
And I will move past you,
Yes it was my mistake
To believe and faith upon you.
Who are you, a villain ?
To do whatever you can !
Tell me the truth,
And I will move from you, man !
Deepening my wounds,
You had set fire on them
My trust on you
And I found myself in shame.
Who do you think ?
To help me as a play
The sinister will rise,
And will ground you in clay.
You broke me, my hopes
My love and innocent desires,
And I promise to burn you

And nobody would be there to care.

5. Playcard

Looking with the hope
Glowing faces and spirits up,
For being together forever,
Finding you a beautiful lover.
Thousand dreams had I created
Thousand wishes had I made,
For the one ,you, for whom,
I let my tears shed.
Memories flashes back,
And conspicuous thoughts that link,
Blinding by your overwhelming love
I forget the world with a blink
Nudging you your sweet touch,
Gathering you in my soft clutch,
Forgetting all the world in vain,
But at last you left me in pain.
Yes, blinded by you in all aspects,
Was with you although being desperate,
Believing you your quixotic words,
But you miscreant used me as a play card.

6. Some had come, some had gone

Some had come ,
And some had gone .
With the waves of the time ,
Like rook and pawn.
The river has died ,
The leaves had torn,
The humanity had ended ,
Where the time goes on.
But there just lives,
A small flicker of ray.
To unturn everything,
That's gonna come on way.
Close your eyes,
And feel that LOVE .
Never changes from sweet to lime,
Even in the perishable wave of time.
Some had come ,
And some had gone,
But I just know You ,
Will stay with me life long ...

7. Smile

Mesmerising someone,
Spreads a smile on my face.
With vibrant colours on,
And it beats faster with pace.
Searching you, for what I tend,
Breezes that blow with glee.
But nowhere what I longed to see,
Even across the farthest ends.
There, you came
like knight in shining armour,
Uplifted my spirits,
And fulfilled with glamour.
Nothing more and nothing less,
To know me what you are,
Leading me a beautiful life,
Sailing me so far.
Nourish me with love,
And cherish me with care
Oh ! What a resplendent you are
My heart beats with Desire

8. Silence

Life is not seen anymore,
the heart aches from the deep core.
Shattered dreams, pieces of glasses,
Which is not mean anymore.
Fear, is what engulfs over all,
obstructs me from my soul.
the darkness covers the world,
Cry, and afraid to fall.
Perfection is not achieved by all,
Mistakes what I did , I regret.
time is not gonna come back,
it's just a matter of fate.
Just believing in peace,
With cool blowing chilly breeze.
Love and cherish silence,
Where I wish , to lie with ease.
Suffering has all enough,
Eyes threaten to spill tears.
Small heart aches from what it bears,
just to leave behind all the fears.
Hope one day I could,
Just the way , moon shine
The silence , I glorify,

Can it bring me divine ?

9. Happiness

Some changes We love , we cry , we laugh and miss
and even want it back !
To evoke , we are lost in words !
Badly we suffer from the past bliss
But we are lost ; in the world's gamble ,
In the deck of cards !
Some enthral , mesmerise their loved ones,
No matter even if they are far apart
The pure souls, still ignites ,
with a new dawn of hope in their hearts.
And the moment I got you
I knew I'm correct
I knew I'm true getting you
My happiness , that you dilate.
And I had known I'll ever
Be happy together,
Ever if a decade passes
I'll wait for a happily ever after.

10. Dried leaf

Living life as a dried leaf,
As without water, a useless ship !
For me, you are my sail,
You are priceless, no rich , no cheap.
I know, today we may be lost,
Maybe wounded, but love the most.
May not be seeing each other,
But, not losing at any cost.
Imperfect, but still adore,
Trust you, always and more.
Glorify you with love,
Dream of you from my heart's core.
We may fall,but stand still,
Get mad at,but laugh and chill,
Lightens moods by goofy faces,
Euphoric memories cloud my will.
Living life as a dried leaf,
As without you ! A useless ship.
Just need the flicker of Hope,
You ! Priceless, no more, no cheap...

11. Shattered

Once I seemed to
Fly with glee,
Having you with me,
Enjoyed what I see.
In our ups and downs,
I laughed and cried,
Watered your soul,
When the storms had dried.
Remained with you,
Although pricking the thorns,
Supported you ,
In your every mourns.
Since never thought,
Whether the sticks could backfire,
With dazzling flame,
Drained all my hopes'n Desires.
Shattered my affection,
With the thorns of word.
Broke my bond,
Just like blowing a
Deck of card.

12. Promise

The days of sweet dreams,
Can never be capable to suffice,
My tenderness for you ,
The blaze burns with avarice.
Under the magnificent tree,
I hold it with true humane,
Sharing my feelings for you,
That rapidly drives me insane.
One promise I would make to you,
To care and nourish you,
To never leave your side,
Just to safe and assure you.
One promise I would make,
To hold you up in your deeds ,
Just like the fluorescent crack of dawn
To fight for you in needs.
One promise I would love to say,
You are my aurora of my way,
Love and care for you ,
With gentle blows that sway.
One promise I would make you clear
Just You are my only endear,
Just keep it in mí vidá ,

My relish proclivity,
It’s all you , everything I swear.

13. Life

I came and I went,
Don't know who noticed.
I lived and I went,
Like nobody felt, I exist .
Like a sparkle, I came
And befriended with you all,
Suddenly,the days ended,
Felt like drastic free fall.
I enlightened you though,
With my kindness and love.
Helped you although,
You there , always shove.
Nothing that I'm in vexation,
Nothing that I'm in rage.
I'm content, helping you all
Like peace, of saints and sage.
I'm what I'm now,
By accruing all the changes,
May people like it or not,
But then, it had crossed all its ranges.
I like it now , to face
Back to my life, entangling mesh,
I like it now to know,

Now in reality, life is a race.

14. Desire

Shh! Don't look up there
The howling winds,
When the two of them ,
Intermingling within a piece of hem.
Shh! Don't shout uff.
The lights are off ,
When she sways her curve
And pulls on his top.
The glorious nights
Passes with a pleasure blur ,
And they wake up
With a desire for glamour.

15. Last breath

She closed her eyes,
and shed a single tear,
On his lap, a lifeless beauty,
taking his endear.
The autumn died,
the Darkness reigned,
while the moon cried,
She closed her eyes,
her lips parted,
and his heart pained.
There he remained,
Frozen, for his loss,
a soul he loved,
Is now lifeless
devoid of her gloss.
He hugged her,
For whom he lived,
And laid his last breath,
For a love, he believed.

16. Thoughts (for him)

I thought you were here,
Within the stars , within the sky,
But I could see the dust ,
That went up and still fly,
I thought you were here,
Hearing me from the soil,
But they were just pebbles,
and created a turmoil.
I thought all favoured me,
to get you, lemme see.
But those were just statues,
had no heart to anybody.
I thought I could touch you,
and let you feel the love,
but those were just ashes,
flew along with your shadow.
I thought I could imagine,
holding hands and enjoying,
This is a glorious dream
provoking my inner to scream.
I thought now, could be near you
Then again I was wrong,
Flooded out to a place,

New home, a town of new.
I wish you could be here,
Holding me tight, holding me near.
I thought I could shed a tear,
Thinking of you, my endear.

17. Homeless

Life without you,
Is just like
The dried petals,
Seeming lifeless,
Those beautiful ways,
Now stretched endless
Oh ! My smile !
Just fake , emotionless
Screaming in rage,
But alas! Voiceless
Living life, just hopeless,
‘cause I called you home,
And now, I’m Homeless.

18. Envy

I envy you,
As a friend you were for me
I envy you ,
Who tore us away, letting me see.
Mesmerising memories of us,
Is that friendship still a lie ?
I still remember how you defy
When anybody violates,
and on you, I rely.
Now it seems to be gone
With a huge reminiscence of tide,
Now just the ashes left
I think I'm bound to abide.
The friendship I dreamt
But here we are apart ,
Thinking of you , I painfully shy,
When I came here
It was rather a goodbye.

19. Voiceless

When my eyes opened
I found them locked
And wandered in the darkness
Still thrilled and shocked.
I wished to awake all night
Just to see you in case
I wished I could Lavish my time
Bouncing with my hair in mesh.
Struggling to find here a confidante
To apprise my own voices
I felt to share
The small weird choices
Somewhere I think
To go on a ride
Under the moonlight
With the light rays beside.
Somewhere I think
The tranquil In my stifle days
Remains close as the wind sways
Letting me know
In my Voiceless page.

20. I wish

I feel to wander
around the trees and lie
I feel so shallow
just breathe and shy.
I wish to smile
But those lips deny me
I wish to gaze
But the eyes don't lemme see.
I feel to wander
just as a girl with glee
Still enduring life
And bend with plea.
Wishing with the wishing star,
I'd love to sail you afar,
The curves tracing the contour
Behind those leaves
I wish one day I'd find
My happy demeanour.

21. Rust

Lost are the days
Of bright shiny rays
When flowers bloomed
The grass swayed.
I felt heavenly
With you dear friend
But all perished
As you turned it to end.
Who are you now
A stranger in the shadows ?
Me, wandering around
For you in meadows.
A pained look
But who is to blame?
I'm the one
With a fragile frame.
Nothing left to say
As everything is lost
Once our friendship
Now it's Rust.

22. Beauty

Alone in the world
Under the dark night sky
Staring above and she shies
Emptiness stings like thorns
Where she shut her tearful eyes
Delicate like a tender leaf
When a tear falls down her cheek
A hole remains in her, still
for the world , she is a stunning fleek.
Contradicting her showing smile,
Glowing under the moonlight night
Constellations as her jewel beads
Such beauty is a wonderful sight.
Desolate girl , wandering around
Within the woods , where trees surround
Hoping for a tint of joy
Alone, with the starry night sky.

23. Rage

I'm walking on an endless way
With a deteriorated body
The waves splashing water
The forest wildly sway.
The raindrops seem like fire
Burning holes in me
The sky turns red
The rage in it , I see.
The gigantic tides form
And block my wobbling frame
Washing me to the shore
Throwing me to inflame.
The world turns against it
Pushing me in pit
Still with burning holes I'm
Forcing myself to knit
Still in a deteriorated body
I'm spinning in an endless day
Where the forest wildly sway
And I'm dead without a say.

24. Alone

What is the value
When her smile is drained
What does it mean
When her face is pained
May she look flawless
Like a glow of winter
Even her colour
Like masterpiece of a painter
Still she's alone
Passing her days
Mourning quietly
Under the moonlit rays
Her eyes wanting someone
To talk to her endlessly
But no-one in the busy world
She is suffering helplessly
Sitting near the window
sobbing in her silent voice
Looking at the moon
without a choice.

25. Conveying love (Moon)

Lost are the days, when
I walked along at night
You seemed smiling
Glowing with your moonlight
Watching you with silent eyes
I found you alluring
Even with the craters
You seemed to me appealing.

26. Wait

Wait ! The time just stop
I wish it listens my voice
Wait ! rewind my joyous days
I wish I'd got a choice.
Time fades , erasing memories
It's goes leaving just the stories
Some day we'd all forget
The past moments without worries.

27. Not everyone is okay

She's sitting at the edge
In agony and pain
Starring at the clouds
At the droplets of rain.
Her body's numb
But still she's bold
Nothing can she feel
Although it's cold.
Dragging herself all way
Hopes to just lie down
But smiles with perfection
And spends her whole day.
Her lips trembles
To talk with a beam
But she's quiet
Lonely without him
Lost alone with the thoughts
Replaying the wanted memories
Not even a good night wish
She sleeps with needful worries.

28. Freezing

Silence is just a pain
Which I feel in intense
Smile is just on the face
While my soul is in vain.
Disastrous are the days
I'm passing without a say
Sleeping with teary eyes
Just moving on my way.
Maybe I'm just insane
With someone I used to talk
Endless laugh seems like ages
But days turned into ugly rock
Freezing with loneliness
And unable to bear
Uncontrollable Affliction
No-one to hear.

29. Drained

I had lost my strength
Millions of words
But sitting dumb
Swallowing it hard,
But feeling numb
Query to whom
When nobody would care
Say it to whom
When no one to share
Trembling from inside
I'm just pained
Shutting my eyes
I see
My colour is drained.

30. Do you know

Do you know ?
I'm watching the same sky,
In the same direction,
and no-one is nearby.
The same constellation
Under the moon's ray,
And the stars twinkle,
Just the same way
But still it's different,
Cause where I'm standing
Do you know ?
I'm still wandering !
Nothing is same as then,
But we both look up,
Our paths changed for sure
Watching the same sky
I know, it's our only cure.

31. Forlorn

I can't stop anymore,
The flood of tears that flow.
I can't smile anymore,
Seeing the sweet fireflies that glow.
I can't hear anymore,
The chirping sounds at night.
I can't see anymore,
The sky, illuminating with starlight.
I can't live anymore,
Tons of secrets to bear.
I can't hold anymore,
Forlorn tears, flowing lavishly,
Starving for their endear.

32. Star

My token of peace
You, my shining star,
Gently blowing breeze,
Like pinpoints, bright and afar.
Closing my eyes in silence
And let anxiety rise and fall
Wishing for dreams to engulf,
I'm just an innocent small girl.
How bright ! magnificent star,
With starlight falling all around,
And between the dark night,
You survive and tempt that surround.
I wish to be like you,
With energetic rays of light,
Love to find my reality,
Falling under your bright sight.
Inspiring courage of yours
Enlighten the darkest of souls,
Protecting the world with shine,
And encouraging me in my falls.

33. Snow

Although the glittery stars surround,
I find myself jailed all around
I don't know what to say but,
Your moonlight supports a lot.
Everytime I pass through the road,
I find myself starring you,
You erase the loneliness I suffer,
And make me appear completely new.
Under your shed, I feel
comfortable silence , what I need.
No matter what others say,
I can hear your unspoken voices indeed.
I'm flowing against the current,
Resting under your warm gaze,
A faint smile I flash, as you shine up,
Still I'm jailed, and tired of hope.
Want to be freed,
although when I don't know !
Tired, but I can't surrender today,
As the dawn would break with flakes of snow.

34. Dust

The leaf is dried now,
With a brown cover on it.
The tree is bald now,
As the leaves fell in pit.
The flowers shrunk,
Hiding their shiny case.
Me too sitting here,
On a dusty rust surface.
Life burnt down slowly,
Consumed by loneliness.
Colour faded away,
Wilting with hopelessness.

35. Nothing left

Nothing left to say,
When my words are sealed.
Needless to speak aloud,
When my voices are sealed.
The smiles I showed,
we're dry and fake,
Yet I believed one day
It'll be from my shake.
Needless to show,
The tearful eyes of mine,
Cause nobody was true,
They just changed with time.

36. Quiet

It’s just I talk a lot
Should I keep quiet ?
I’d seal my lips,
Then would it be alright ?
Thinking that I should laugh
a lot, to hide my frown
still I'm afraid of thoughts
a fear of getting torn.
I should then fake my smile
to hide my agony and pain
I should quiet myself
To stop those, melting in vain.

37. Are you sure ?

Are you sure of it ?
To laugh without care,
Without any frown
and no miseries to share !
Are you sure of it ?
to those you speak
they smile back bright
even when they know
they have sorrows to fight !
Are you sure of it ?
that you're not in a deceive
Do you like it ?
The way you still live.

38. Crimson blaze

Oh ! I see,
In crimson red,
Melodies with the birds,
Silk cotton flowers surround,
they chirp sweetly all around.
They said they love me,
To the heart's core.
It's the sweet truth ?
Or just a lie,
waiting to get sour?
Oh ! I see , they flew away,
When my flowers withered.
They went away,
When i was alone, shattered.
I was a brown log,
Stood in winter frost.
Still smiling to them,
For the Ruby they lost.
Oh ! I see ,
A sparrow is with me,
chirped spring to come,
Stood by me when I was glum.

Oh ! I see
It was a sweet truth,
The spring bloomed,
So do my flowers.
The birds were stunned,
Stupefied with every gaze.
There I was smiling,
With my velvet crimson blaze.

39. Regrets

To all your miseries
Is there any end ?
To all your expressions
Is there any point to pretend ?
You suffer in agony and pain
Like drought , absence of rain
It's true and you go insane
Hoping solitude, wandering lane.
Laugh ! it's not what you should
Until you find back the way
Just race and run
Until you do whatever you say .
You can't feel your wrongdoings
until the time is gone
You cry and regret
Alas! nothing can be undone.

40. Lost

It is really worth,
For people to feel worthless?
or is it necessary to give up,
and become hopeless?
Seeing the world moving fast,
and no-one beams anymore.
are they really capable to move,
Without getting numb and sore ?
Let us find a quiet place,
closing our eyes, sitting for a while,
Can we bring back the lost riches,
And wholeheartedly smile ?

41. Eating up my soul

Holding the keys,
I'm shivering,
thinking about
opening the doors,
I'm fumbling
to find the right one.
But then I was lucky
to get it all Wrong.
The key which i put in
didn't "clank" the lock.
My heart seized in terror,
So suffocating, so freezing
pale complexion, rigid skin
growing in utter coldness.
Jamming my veins
Blood wants to ooze out,
Withering my remnants.
Slowly eating up my soul.
I'm holding up the keys,
In Front of "still" closed door
as my soul break down
Squeaking in tremor.

42. Year's end

It's the year's end,
But why is it so cold ? Is it because
of December ? Or due to the void within me ?
It's the year's end.
But why do I feel the hush of wind ?
Is it making me aware of my destruction?
Or allowing me to be free like itself?
It's cold again, my feet are numb
My face reflects pale white
But i need to wake up again
With a wide smile.
Anger and hatred, is it okay for me
To carry it all alone ?
To compress the void within me ?
Can it heal this way ?
It's the end again
Why am I so cold
Is is because of winter or due to
The happy people near me
Making me aware of my Hollow presence?

43. A short encounter

I was a lonely passerby
Walking down a lane
When I saw her peeping
From a dusty window pane.
A warm breeze blew
Her eyes widened with furrowed brow
I saw her face, when she pout
Stretched her hands but ,
Her amber hat flew out .
Creeped out of the square frame ,
She was small, still ran to acclaim,
Dusting her golden fabric,
She smelled of aspartame.
Taking her belongings in captivity,
She quietly turned around,
And saw me staring her ,
She smiled, vast profound.
I was a lonely passerby,
Walking down a lane.
The sight of her beauty,
Pulled my heart to abstain.
smiles exchanged and crossed paths,
I slowly walked on my way

It was nothing but a beauty
A short encounter, they say.

44. Mistake

Not to give up, I fear,
Thinking of the disastrous past,
With the loss I bear,
Thinking if it would overlast.
Did mistakes what in realise,
But it is not what we should criticise,
The burns I got what I feel,
Maybe tomorrow, it will be precise.
Still today, fighting my demons,
Hope once to be cured at all,
Tired of what I realised my past,
Feel like jumping and just free fall.
But neither my fault,
To be quit at all,
Nor yours towards me to fall,
The destiny is destined, and what we call,
But that intentionally made me crawl.
Made up my mind just,
To go forward and,
Move on where I can stand,
It is not what to fear!
And I think I can bear,
And can lead my life I swear.

45. Mirror

Break me please!
You pulled me back
Towards you
Cherished me as gem,
Making me feel new.
Can you keep it?
The 'me' lacked fear.
Can you take it?
The 'me' beyond mirrors.
You burned on the light,
Putting me on my feet,
Still cared to carry;
As if, a bleak sheet?
Then, you didn't know
Who was I; still shine.
Now, you realised my demon,
How can you come and rest,
Claiming you're mine?
How can you join
The broken puzzled line
Remaining the same you're
Years ago?
How can you warn

My heart, the way you did
Years ago?

46. Starlight

When I looked at you,
With a blush on my face,
Oh! The charming beauty,
Stop me in each place.
The time I walked around,
ah! caught your prettiest sight,
As if I'm a solivagant girl,
And you showed me
the splendid Starlight.
I love the bluish nights,
'cause I clearly see you in case,
And too your bright Ray's,
That spotifies my ways
Oh! What a life without you,
Only stone hearts could survive a few
Without your twinkling shines,
And, I unlike those,
Which could be crushed and blew.
The blush in my face still continues,
When I looked at you with bright sight
It really gives me immense pleasure,
With your glorious beauty of Starlight.

47. Bliss

I wish to have gone away,
to spend every single day.
splendicious your glorious beauty,
that I'm short of words to say.
No one awaits like the blush of fire,
for the inner voices to say,
But I'm here with a desire
to feel the smallest, without delay.
The time comes to nurture and flourish,
and I'm here to enjoy with you, a bliss.
I know that I'm not alone to sway,
as you are beside me every day.
The nights are full of darkness,
And the cold that surrounds,
I love the moment you create
the lovely fireflies that light all around.
And I feel the best way,
shall eagerly be near you.
And watching your sparkling beauty.
shall always try to praise you.

48. Devine

Who are you,
your creation is just unimaginable,
with the glorious beauty all around,
And my attraction always grew.
When i am depressed,
the place you provide,
to overcome the grief.
with proper care of me beside.
A single touch of you
can have the greeneries
and all that everything we need,
with LOVE, indeed.
When the surroundings are covered with darkness,
and i lose my belief,
you are magnificent,
with a bright ray of hope and relief.
Who are you,
To serve for me day and night,
and now going far forever
with a blinking gloomy ray of light.

49. Reality

Wandering here and there,
Always try to find where you are,
But vigorously miss those days,
Which I enjoyed once with care.
Imagining a lot of things,
Although knowing,
it can never be
But faiths can ever come with wings.
Which I love to see.
Don't want a busy life,
And want to come near you.
Before your greeneries squeeze and dry,
Hoping I could preserve a few.
The prettiest sight, I still remember,
The way I slept on your lap,
The drunken memories with you
When you let me pause and take a nap.

50. Throbbing heart

I can see it, in front of me,
Why can't I touch it ? Is it that hard ?
I look down, and see our distance,
Is it really far to walk along and catch ?
I gasp for air, why so suffocating ?
Is it that hard to breathe ?
Did my presence scare you ?
That you took me and tried to crumple ?
Yes, you're successful, you won me !
Are you satisfied now, seeing me unstable ?
I was happy, living in solitude.
You found me, letting me feel precious.
But you didn't hesitate to break me,
Although I was gracious !
Do you think you know, how much
the hurt within me still ignites,
The flashes still tearing
Do you think you know, how much
I thrived for you,
still it was in vain
My throbbing heart,
shatter in pain.

Is It Okay For Me ?

Can I close my eyes now ?
    in peace, dreaming about something,
    I used to do before ?
    Is it okay to feel the wramth again ?

The End

In the end, why is it cold again ?
Is it due to december, or due to the void in my heart ?
why am I so cold now ?
Is it because people are happy,
near me, while I fake a smile ?
Still i wish to move forward,
To achieve what I lost
and gain what has always been mine.

9 798889 867562

Printed by Libri Plureos GmbH in Hamburg, Germany